Enjoy!
Linda
2011

NEW MEXICO
portrait of a state

NEW MEXICO

portrait of a state

DAVID MUENCH

GRAPHIC ARTS BOOKS

All photographs © MMVII by David Muench, except as noted:
pages 4–5, 20–21, 25, 27, 39, 51, 55, 56, 60–61, 73, 76–77,
78, 81, 87, 96, and 99 © MMVII by Marc Muench;
page 98 © MMVII by Zandria Muench Beraldo;
page 64 © MMVII by Mistral Images/IndexOpen.com;
page 65 © MMVII by Walter Bibikow/DanitaDelimont.com.

All rights reserved. No part of this book may be reproduced or
transmitted in any form or by any means, electronic or mechanical,
including photocopying, recording, or by any information storage
and retrieval system, without written permission of the publisher.

Library of Congress Control Number: 2006926478
International Standard Book Number: 978-1-55868-990-9

Captions and book compilation © MMVII by
Graphic Arts Books, an imprint of
Graphic Arts Center Publishing Company
P.O. Box 10306, Portland, Oregon 97296-0306
503/226-2402; www.gacpc.com

The five-dot logo is a registered trademark of
Graphic Arts Center Publishing Company.

President: Charles M. Hopkins
Associate Publisher: Douglas A. Pfeiffer
Editorial Staff: Timothy W. Frew, Kathy Howard, Jean Bond-Slaughter
Production Coordinator: Heather Doornink
Cover Design: Elizabeth Watson
Interior Design: Jean Andrews

Printed in the United States of America

FRONT COVER: ◗ Shiprock, standing
in the high desert on the Navajo Reservation, is
sacred to the Navajos, who call it *Tse Bi Dahl,* meaning "Rock
with Wings." It is a symbol for New Mexico, "The Land of Enchantment."
BACK COVER: ◗ La Ventana Arch, New Mexico's second-largest, spans 135 feet.
◄◄ The Rio de las Trampas meets up with the Embudo River to help drain
the Pecos Wilderness, the second-largest wilderness area in the state. In 1964,
Pecos became part of the National Wilderness Preservation System.
◄ At dawn, the massive Shiprock seems to sail across the landscape.
► Parts of Carlsbad Caverns are marked by huge
"pillars" that seem to hold up the ceiling.

◄ La Ventana Natural Arch forms a window over-
looking El Malpais National Conservation Area. Established
in 1987, El Malpais is managed by the Bureau of Land Management.
▲ At Pueblo Bonito, an ancient kiva, a place where sacred ceremonies
were held, lies within Chaco Culture National Historical Park.

▲ A big sky spreads majestically over
Table Mesa, in New Mexico's northwest corner.
A mesa is a naturally occurring flat elevation that
rises above the surrounding landscape.

▲ Winter snow envelops San Francisco de Asís
Mission Church in Ranchos de Taos. Named for St. Francis
of Assisi, who lived from A.D. 1182 to 1226, the mission is built
like a fortress, with thick adobe walls and buttresses.

▲ Yucca, such as this one in the
Organ Mountains, is the state flower of New Mexico.
► Petroglyphs, carvings or inscriptions etched into rocks, dot the
Three Rivers Petroglyph Site, protected by the Bureau of Land Management.
►► Situated on a knoll that rises above the mesa top, Citadel
Ruin is accessible only via a rough ladder.

◄ In summer, asters and sunflowers blanket a high meadow
beneath the Sierra Blanca, also called the White Mountains.
▲ The Diamond A Ranch is in New Mexico's boot heel.

15

▲ The Sangre de Cristo Mountains are the
southernmost sub-range of the Rocky Mountains.
The name means "blood of Christ."

▲ Winter blankets the Sandia Mountains in the
Cibola National Forest. Most of the range is situated within
the nearly two-million-acre Cibola National Forest, which incorporates
and protects ecosystems that range from desert to prairie,
from piñon-juniper to subalpine spruce and fir.

▲ An 1880 Navajo weaving, from
the traditional period, hangs at the Museum
of Indian Arts and Culture in Santa Fe.

▲ Corn and chilis, Pueblo
staples, dry on a door frame.
►► Hondo Chute, outside the Taos Ski Valley
pistes, is a challenging experience.

◄ The Great Kiva of the ancient Pueblo
Bonito is the most celebrated and investigated site
in Chaco Canyon, Chaco Culture National Historical Park.
▲ A balloon flies over rocks of Petroglyphs National Monument.
The annual Albuquerque International Balloon Fiesta® attracts
thousands of balloonists from all over the world.

▲ El Santuario de Chimayo, built between 1814 and 1816,
sits near the site where a crucifix miraculously appeared.
► Archbishop Jean Baptiste Lamy commissioned the St. Francis
Cathedral in 1869. He is buried beneath it.

◄ A snow-covered Douglas fir tree sits near the top
of 10,678-foot Sandia Crest. Visitors have easy access via the
world's longest tramway to an observation deck at the 10,378-foot level.
▲ Aspen Heights is located in the Santa Fe National Forest.
►► A winter sunrise in the Black Range reveals the
Organ Mountains on the distant horizon.

◄ An adobe façade in Cerrillos, situated just south of
Santa Fe, shows the simple beauty of a traditional village.
▲ Petroglyphs have been etched into rock
in New Mexico's Abo district.

▲ The Rio Pecos heads into the Sangre
de Cristo Mountains, then flows southward
through New Mexico to enter the Rio Grande in Texas.
▶ Grasses are reflected in Bosque del Apache National Wildlife
Refuge. *Bosque del Apache* means "woods of the Apache."

◄ North Taos Pueblo, the largest Pueblo structure
continuously inhabited, nestles beneath Taos Mountain.
▲ A plate is embellished with Zuni-style animal figures.
►► Shiprock displays a double image in Navajo
country after monsoonal rains.

35

▲ Ghost Ranch, a twenty-one-thousand-acre retreat, was home to
Georgia O'Keeffe from 1949 until her death in 1986 at the age of ninety-eight.
▶ Skiers have to hike up 12,481-foot Kachina Peak, in the Sangre de Cristo
Mountains, in order to ski down. It is said that Ernie Blake, founder of
the Taos Ski Valley, refused to build a lift up the mountain,
claiming Americans were too lazy.

◄ A ghostly formation in New Cave, Carlsbad Caverns
National Park, appeared in the 1985 movie *King Solomon's Mines.*
▲ The best known of the 113 caves in Carlsbad Caverns
is the Big Room, which covers 8.2 acres.

▲ Prickly poppies brighten Capulin Volcano National Monument.
► Pedestal erosions are a prominent feature of the Bisti Badlands.
►► Acoma Pueblo was built on top of a 367-foot sandstone mesa to
protect the town from enemies. It is claimed that this seventy-acre
village, established in the twelfth century or even earlier, is the
oldest continuously inhabited city in the United States.

◄ A lone yucca flourishes in the gypsum sand of
White Sands National Monument. The national monument
protects some 275 square miles of the unique white sand dunes.
▲ Capulin Mountain, a large cinder cone, rises about a thousand feet above
the surrounding plains in Capulin Volcano National Monument.

▲ Paintbrush and astors brighten a meadow
in the Brazos Mountains. Paintbrush, also known
as prairie-fire, includes some two hundred species.
Astors often show up in shades of purple.

▲ Star trails fill the sky above City of Rocks in
southern New Mexico. The City of Rocks State Park was
established in 1952. Situated at an elevation of 5,200 feet, the
"city" consists of rock columns rising as high as forty
feet, separated by lanes that resemble city streets.

▲ Jemez State Monument, designated in
1935, includes Towa pueblo and massive Spanish mission ruins.
► Opened in 1917, Santa Fe's Museum of Fine Arts promotes Southwest art and artists.
►► Pueblo Bonito, in Chaco Culture National Historical Park, was once a thriving
community. The Chaco Culture dates from about A.D. 850 through 1150.

◄ A camposanto sits below the
snow-covered Brazos Mountains.
▲ A corral in northern New Mexico
shows the area's rural history.

▲ Jagged peaks of the Sandia Mountains rise above brilliant fall color.
▶ Pecos began in about A.D. 800, and over time, the Indian pueblo became
the largest in the Southwest. The Misión de Nuestra Señora de Los Angeles de
Porciuncula de los Pecos, in Pecos National Historical Park, was constructed in
the early 1600s but had to be rebuilt in the latter part of the century
after it was destroyed in an Indian uprising. The church
ruins rise behind a piece of ancient pottery.

57

◄ The Rio Chama Wilderness encompasses more
than fifty thousand acres in northwest New Mexico.
▲ Early morning fog crawls across the Rio Grande Bosque.
►► At sunset, a tree-lined ridge appears on fire.

▲ Peñasco Blanco is an arc-shaped Chaco
Culture compound built over a period of some two
hundred years, beginning perhaps around A.D. 900. The
rock wall, including a window, still shows the careful work
that went into creating such a substantial structure.

▲ A kiva gives a glimpse into life in Pueblo Bonito,
which was constructed in Chaco Canyon over a thousand-
year period by Ancestral Puebloans. The oldest parts
of Chaco date back to about A.D. 850.

▲ Christmas decorations
brighten a doorway on De Vargas
Street in Santa Fe.

▲ Mountain men and Native American traders fill
the courtyard of the Palace of the Governors in Santa Fe
with their wares during the annual August buffalo roast.
Here, Indian pattern blankets are offered for sale.

▲ Datura, called both angel's trumpet and devil's trumpet, blooms before the Organ Mountains. The mountains received their name because people thought the vertical rock formations resembled the pipes of an organ.

▲ Corrales still retains much of its rural character.
►► In 1907, President Theodore Roosevelt signed a proclamation
establishing the cliff dwellings at Gila as a national monument.

▲ The Animas River enters New Mexico
from Durango, Colorado. Rafters, canoers, and
kayakers enjoy the river year-round.

▲ Sandhill cranes *(Grus canadensis)* congregate along the Rio Grande. Several areas along the river provide stops for the cranes on their migrations.

▲ Fort Union was established in 1851 as the guardian
of the Santa Fe Trail. Wagons in need of repair were taken to
the Mechanics Corral, constructed of adobe with a stone foundation.

▶ Built between 1760 and 1776, the church in Las Trampas was originally called
Santo Tomás, but the name was changed in 1881 to San José de Gracia.

◄ Named the county seat in 1884,
the mining town of Hillsboro is not quite a
ghost town today. A museum displays historic artifacts.
▲ The wood-and-adobe opera house hints of better
times at the old mining town of Pinos Altos.
►► Taos Ski Village displays its magic.

▲ Alcove House, formerly known as
Ceremonial Cave, was used by Ancestral
Puebloans more than seven hundred years ago.
Situated outside of Santa Fe, the cave is now
part of Bandelier National Monument.

▲ Petroglyphs are found in many parts
of New Mexico. This one was pecked into rock
along the banks of the Lower Rio Grande.

▲ Autumn grasses brighten the plains before the
Sangre de Cristo, one of the longest mountain chains on
earth. The range includes ten peaks over 14,000 feet high.
▶ A cottonwood trunk forms a textured backdrop
for an aspen leaf in the Brazos Mountains.

◄ Pueblo Bonito is the largest
and most famous ruin in Chaco Canyon.
▲ The Great Kiva of Casa Rinconada, in Chaco
Culture National Historical Park, is part of the largest,
most architecturally advanced of all ancient Southwestern villages.
▶▶ The Plains of St. Augustine are carpeted in wildflowers.
Very Large Array dishes line the horizon.

◄ The Big Hatchet Mountains are a
small, rugged range in New Mexico's boot heel.
▲ Autumn graces the granite cliffs of the Sandia
Mountains, viewed from the tramway.

▲ Paintbrush and yucca blend together,
seeming to form a new species in Kiowa
National Grassland, near Clayton.

▲ The interior of Gila Cliff Dwellings
was home to Mogollon people during
the eleventh and twelfth centuries.

▲ The sand dunes in Rio Grande Valley
take on a golden hue beneath the Organ Mountains.
▶ Tumbleweeds create an intricate design before the Cooks Range.
▶▶ Quarai was a thriving pueblo in 1598 when Oñate arrived
to claim the territory for Spain. The Salinas Pueblo
Missions were constructed of native red brick.

▲ Rabbitbrush thrives beside the
Jemez River. The Jemez affords white-
water rafting along some fifty miles of its length.
▶ Yarrow, penstemon, and paintbrush flourish
in the cracks of a rock on Sandia Crest.

◄ At Kasha-Katuwe Tent Rocks National
Monument, the unique shapes of the rocks were
created by volcanism and erosion. The cone-shaped rock
formations are wind- and water-eroded pumice and tuff deposits.
The tent rock formations vary from a few feet to ninety feet in height.
▲ An abandoned adobe structure slowly gives way to
weather and time in Claunch, Socorro County.

▲ Chili peppers decorate a fence in Albuquerque.
► Cliff dwellings in Gila Cliff Dwellings National Monument
shed light on the lives of people of the Mogollon Culture who
lived in the Gila Wilderness. The surroundings probably look
today much like they did when the cliff dwellings were inhabited.
►► Yucca stands out against a brilliant sunset in Hachita Valley.

◄ Honey mesquite blooms in the plains beneath
the Organ Mountains after a summer thunderstorm.
▲ Fall color takes over the Brazos Mountains.

▲ Prickly pear cactus blooms in City of Rocks State Park.
► Valle Grande, also known as the Valles Caldera and the Jemez
Caldera, is a scenic area in the Jemez Mountains. It is part of what was once
a supervolcano that erupted in ancient times, an eruption
that helped shape the Jemez Mountains.

◄ Cane cholla flourishes beside the Rio
Pecos. "West of the Pecos" became a reference to
the Wild West frontier in the latter half of the 1800s.
▲ Red claret cup cactus and creamy yucca create a colorful
tableau on the plains in front of the Organ Mountains.
►► At sunset, the sands of White Sands National
Monument stretch to the horizon.

107

▲ Pueblo del Arroyo, protected in Chaco Culture National
Historical Park, was built from about A.D. 1025 to A.D. 1125.
► The Cimarron River is known as the Dry Cimarron in New
Mexico, because it sometimes disappears entirely under the riverbed.
►► The Gran Quivira church ruins in Salinas National Monument attest
to a history of Christian missions. Once a vibrant community called
Las Humanas, Gran Quivira began to decline in the 1600s.